Teacher Appreciation Gift

Made in the USA
Coppell, TX
04 May 2022

77405745R00059